An Okie Saga

Vernon L. Lawson

authorHOUSE®

AuthorHouse™
1663 Liberty Drive, Suite 200
Bloomington, IN 47403
www.authorhouse.com
Phone: 1-800-839-8640

This book is a work of non-fiction. Unless otherwise noted, the author
and the publisher make no explicit guarantees as to the accuracy of
the information contained in this book and in some cases, names of
people and places have been altered to protect their privacy.

© 2008 Vernon L. Lawson. All rights reserved.

No part of this book may be reproduced, stored in a retrieval system, or
transmitted by any means without the written permission of the author.

First published by AuthorHouse 4/17/2008

ISBN: 978-1-4343-4296-6 (sc)
ISBN: 978-1-4343-4297-3 (hc)

Library of Congress Control Number: 2007908875

Printed in the United States of America
Bloomington, Indiana

This book is printed on acid-free paper.

I was born on April 23, 1924, in the little town of Porum, Oklahoma, which is in Muskogee County; so you could say, "I'm an Okie from Muskogee."

I can recall most of the events of my life from the time when I was about four years old but can't recall anything prior to that time. We lived on a little farm out in the country from Porum, Oklahoma, where my daddy farmed mostly cotton, corn, and a few peanuts. My mother always had a big garden as we were too poor to buy anything from the store except for the bare essentials like flour, salt, sugar, black pepper, and a few other things.

Remembering back to the winter of 1928, it was very cold with snow on the ground, my sisters and I all bundled up, sitting up in the loft of the barn shelling and eating raw peanuts my father had put there to dry.

There were seven children in our family. I had a sister and brother younger than myself and four older sisters. We lived in a big ol' farmhouse with a storm cellar at the rear of the house. I can still hear my father saying, "Looks like a tornado headed our way; so we had better go to the storm cellar." Sometimes the storm passed us by rather quickly and we didn't have to stay down there very long. Other times we had to sleep down there all night with the mice and, now and then, snakes.

We children all had chores assigned to us. I had to get a few ears of corn from the corncrib every evening and shell them for the chickens. I also threw a few ears into the hog pen as we raised our meat and made our own lard for cooking.

Sometimes my mother fed the pigs. I can see her with a cob of corn in each hand, knocking them together and saying, "soo-ee. Soo-ee," and the pigs came running to her.

The big old house had no indoor plumbing but behind which was an outhouse. We had a well from which we drew water, which was taken, into the house for drinking, cooking, and bathing. My mother heated the water on the big wood cooking stove in the kitchen. Every Saturday night she would bathe us all in a round galvanized washtub.

To this day I remember my mother heating water outside in a big copper boiler and washing all of the clothes in a washtub and using a scrub board to get our clothes clean. She would scrub until her fingers were so sore that they sometimes bled. She would have one or two of the older girls hang them on the clothesline to dry. If we got rips and tears in our clothes, my mother simply sewed them up or patched them as we didn't have any money for new ones. If we were lucky, our mother and dad would take us into town once a year to get some new shoes. If we wore holes in the soles of our shoes before then, we simply cut pieces of cardboard as liners and put them in our shoes to cover the holes.

My daddy farmed all the acreage using two mules, a plow, and harrow. The female mule was named Molly, and the male mule was called Cass. I can still hear him saying at the end of the row he was plowing either, "Haw, Cass," or, "Gee, Cass." I believe "haw" was to turn right and "gee" was to turn left.

My daddy would work all day plowing, and every now and then I would take water to him. At lunchtime my mother would fix a lunch pail for him, and I was elected to take him his lunch. In the summertime all of us children went barefooted. I liked this time of year as I would sometimes follow behind daddy as he was plowing. It felt so good to walk in the soft earth.

When daddy planted cotton, he had an old two-row planter pulled by the mules. It was a different story when he planted corn. My mother and us children had to drop a kernel of corn approximately 6" apart in every row he plowed for corn. We had no mechanical corn planter to do so. It seemed like we were at the job for days, and I was so glad when it was finished.

Mother, who was part Choctaw Indian, was kind-hearted and would give you the shirt off her back. I remember the time two drunken Indians came to the door and wanted food. My mother told them, "Okay. Come in and sit at the big kitchen table," while she cooked them some food. One Indian got to his feet and went looking around the room and started into another room. My mother asked him in Choctaw, his Indian language, what he was looking for. I guess he told her Whiskey because my mother said, "No whiskey," and grabbed a skillet and started hitting him and chased him out of the house. She told the other Indian in Choctaw that if he wanted food she would give it to him but no whiskey.

In the fall my daddy would have some of the neighbor men come over to help him kill and butcher some pigs for meat for the coming year. He would reciprocate and go over to their house and help them do the same. We had a low-fenced runway going to the pigpen. My father would stand upon it with a big sledgehammer in his hands. He would tell me to get in the pigpen and would point to the pig he wanted me to run out. I would do this. As the pig came out the chute and under my dad, he would smack it in the head with a big sledgehammer. The sledgehammer would only stun the pig, and my daddy would jump down and with a big butcher knife slit the throat of the pig. He would then slit a hole in the pig's hind-leg tendons. He had one of the mules all harnessed up with a single tree behind. With the hooks on the single tree, he would secure the pig's hind-feet tendons and pull the pig over to the huge pot of boiling water. Above the big pot was a huge A-frame made out of logs with a pulley and rope. My father would undo the single tree from the mule and hook the single tree to the rope. The men then would pull on the rope and lift the single tree with the pig on it up and over the big pot of water. Then they would slowly douse the pig into the hot water for a minute or two. Then they would hoist the pig out of the water and pull on the pig's hair. If the hair came out easily, then he was ready to scrape. If the hair didn't come off easily, then the pig was doused into the hot water again. The pig was then lifted and put on a big board across some sawhorses. Then the hair was scraped off and the pig was then gutted and cut up into various pieces, i.e., hams, hog's head, chops, bacon, et cetera. This was a good time as we had fresh meat for a week or so. The rest of the meat was salted down and put in wooden barrels to keep from spoiling and placed in the cellar.

Most of the family didn't like to have fried salt pork for breakfast with our biscuits and gravy. I remember my mother to this day soaking the salt pork overnight in water so it wouldn't taste so salty when fried in the morning.

At that time no one had a refrigerator, and when we got a pail or two of milk from old Bessie, we had to keep it cool to prevent curdling or souring. My father had built upon four stilts a frame like a big 4' x 4' box. All over the top and sides were tacked gunnysacks. When the sides were kept wet with water, the milk and anything we put into this "refrigerator" was kept cool a long time. One of my older sisters was assigned to draw water from the well and keep the gunnysacks wet.

As I said before, my mother had a large garden. All of us kids helped her to pick all of the vegetables. She spent a great number of days, also us children, shelling peas and cutting up string beans and cutting the kernels off the cob. My mother would preserve all these in mason jars and then place them in the cellar for future use.

In the wintertime, meat was a little scarce. To this end, my father out of old hollow oak logs made what was called "rabbit gums," or traps. The backs of the traps were blocked off with a piece of wood. The front had a little wooden door that would slide up and down. The top of the door was hooked with a string that was tied to a fulcrum on top of the log. Towards the rear of the log, a small hole was bored through the top. Another string was tied to the other end of the fulcrum, and it went down into the hole inside the trap. This end of the string was tied to a trip mechanism. We put loose corn around this mechanism, and when the rabbits came in to eat the corn, the trip was activated, i.e., the little front door came down, locking the rabbit inside. About every other morning, my father and I would make our rounds to the eight or ten traps. Most of the time on our rounds it had snowed the night before, and we could see the imprints of the little tracks of the snowshoe rabbits leading up to the traps.

One thing that got me a little upset was that when we saw the trap had been tripped, my dad would raise the door a little and reach in and grab whatever was in there. It was always a rabbit, but I kept thinking what if it was a skunk or a 'possum? My dad would hold the rabbit up by its hind feet with one hand. Then he would bring the edge of this other hand down hard behind the ears of the rabbit's head. The rabbit would kick a few times and then would be dead. Then I would put him in the gunnysack that I carried for this purpose. To this day I remember how my daddy made these traps. Since at present we are deluged with ground squirrels eating our garden vegetables and nuts, I built one trap, and it has really proved worthwhile.

Our rounds usually took us past a small creek which ran next to our property. Along the banks grew wild persimmon trees. These permissions were small, and in the winter, they were so sweet to eat if you could beat the 'possums to them. There would be eight or ten 'possums in the trees, and once in a while my dad would bring his gun, and we would have a 'possum for dinner. I didn't like them very much as they were so fat and greasy. Later on something happened, and I would never eat a 'possum after that.

1928 had been a poor year for farming as there was very little rain, and irrigation systems were nonexistent. Dad relied on rain to water our crops. That year the rain hardly fell, and with no water, the corn and cotton didn't make a crop. I think that year we had no money to go to town and buy any new clothes or shoes. Then came 1929, and it was another dry year. In the spring my dad started plowing the ground, and it was so hard with no moisture that he plowed up nothing but clods of earth. Also, while plowing, the mule, Cass, would not obey my father's command to turn. My father carried a gun across the handles of the plow. He became so angry with Cass that he took the rifle and killed him. Then he took all the harness off of Cass, hooked Cass's hind legs to a single tree, and had Molly pull Cass down into a dry wash next to our farm.

Day after day I would go to the bank of the wash and look down at Cass lying there. For the first few days, he got bigger and bigger, or bloated. One day as I looked down, I could see that Cass had popped and I could not believe what I saw.

Since 1929 was going to be another year when we would have no crops, my father and mother decided we would move to California. We sold all the chickens, pigs, cows, mule, and horse and most all the other stuff we owned but not all of the household goods.

My dad went into town – I think it was Stigler, Oklahoma – and bought a new 1929 Ford touring car for around $500. For the next two weeks or so, as we sold all of our things, my father started fixing up our car for the upcoming journey to California. Above the running boards from front fender to rear fender, he took boards approximately 10" wide and bolted it to the fenders so we would have extra space for carrying things. The little car was crammed with pillows, blankets, clothes, et cetera. On the running boards my father carried some tools, a big ax, containers of kerosene, gasoline, oil, and a small tent.

My brother, being about two years old, rode up front with my mom and dad, and the rest of the kids rode in the rear, sitting and laying on the blankets, pillows, and clothes. I would like to reminisce about what we had on the farm before we started our journey. I remember that not too far away from our farm grew some hickory nut trees. The shell of these nuts were as hard as iron, and you had to use a hammer or a big rock to smash them. Some of the meat would come out when smashed, but to get the rest was a chore. To fix this I found a medium-size nail, and with my dad's hammer and a steel surface of some kind, I flattened out the sharp end. With this nail I would pry out the meat left in the hickory nutshells.

Not too far from these trees was a huge pile of flat rocks. It was so rocky that no one could farm there. Here I would sit hour after hour cracking nuts on the flat rocks and eating them. In these rocks lived mountain boomers, which were huge lizards. Once in a while they would come close to me, and being a little frightened, I would start to run away. They would chase after me for some distance and turn back. I would then go back and crack nuts again.

Also not too far from our house was a creek that had deep waterholes in it. Here in the summertime we children would play and swim. Also, on the banks grew wild muscadine grapes that were like concord grapes but with a few more seeds. The grapes would stain your mouth and fingers a bright red, but they were delicious.

Down through the trees were various trails used by cattle and horses. I remember the day two of my older sisters were riding a horse bareback. They were about eight and ten years of age. Ruby, the oldest one, was riding in front while Vivian, the younger one, was riding in back. They were riding lickety-split down through the trees on one of these trails. When they came to a big tree with the branches overhanging the trail, Ruby, riding in front, ducked under the branches, but Vivian, not seeing them, was jerked off the horse by the hair of her head. She lost some of her hair but was not hurt physically.

Not too far away from our house was a swamp-like place which we called "The Bottoms." In this place were many wild pecan trees among which lived a drove of wild pigs. I could not go to "The Bottoms" by myself; so that is why I cracked hickory nuts. Once in a while my older sisters would let me go with them. We would take a couple of gunnysacks to carry our pecans in. When we went into the area, you could hear the pigs grunting and see them rooting in the leaves and earth for the pecans. We would try to steer clear of the pigs, but sometimes they would come close to us, and we would throw big limbs and rocks to drive them away. The reason they came close was because they were drawn to the nuts we had knocked down by throwing limbs up into the trees. After we got about two gunnysacks full, we would go home, and that winter around the big stove in the kitchen we would crack and eat our fill of pecans.

One of the disadvantages of living in the country and near a very small town was there was not a mortuary nearby. If there was a death, it was one or two days before the mortician came to pick up the deceased. In the interim, the neighbors of the deceased would take turns sitting up with the body day and night until the mortician came to pick him up. My father was one of the volunteers and went on duty one afternoon until 12:00 midnight. My dad for whatever reason on his watch tied a rope around the deceased's chest and ran the rope under the sheets, under the rug, and through a partly open window. When he was relieved by the next man, he went outside and stood by the window where the end of the rope lay. The man who relieved him sat in a chair by the deceased's bed. As he began to nod off, my father pulled on the rope, causing the deceased to rise up. The man partly woke up and saw the deceased rising in the bed. He couldn't believe his eyes and started rubbing them. At this my father let the rope go and the deceased lay back down. My father waited for a while longer until the man nodded off again whereupon my father pulled on the rope quite hard, causing the deceased to rise almost vertical in the bed. The man watching awoke, and about that time the deceased fell out of bed. The man ran out of the house and would never sit up with another deceased person again.

Well, we started our journey to California one spring morning. In this little Ford sedan were us six children with our mother and father for a total of eight individuals. My oldest sister, Viola, went to ride with some of our relatives who were also making the same trip. A good part of our trip was made along the old highway, Route 66. Some of the highway was paved, but most of it was a dirt road through the sagebrush. Some of the road was pure sand, and we got stuck now and then. When this happened, we all got out of the car and helped push the car out of the sand. Sometimes it would be stuck so deep that my dad would cut sagebrush and put them under the rear wheels to get traction to help us out of the sand.

Flat tires were another hazard, and we had quite a few. We had a spare tire we could put on, but soon we would have another flat. We would all get out of the car, and my father would put a jack under the wheel with the flat and would raise it up so he could unbolt the wheel off the axle. Then he had to take his tools and get the tire off the rim. He would take the inner tube – no tubeless tires then – out of the tire and get his tube patching kit. He would use his hand pump to partly inflate the tube so he could locate the hole. When he located the hole, he would put a patch on it. This done, the above process was reversed, and we were on our way again.

As we were en route, we would stop and cook something to eat. Mostly we would eat in the car on our way. My dad would stop and buy things to eat like white bread, bologna, cheese, apples, saltine crackers, et cetera.

My sisters and I marveled at the white bread, which we called "light bread," as we had only biscuits before to eat. We called the wheat bread "brown bread," and for years I can remember saying, "Pass the white bread or brown bread," at our kitchen table.

To start our trip, we had very little money, and it was soon gone. When we entered Texas, we had to stop and earn some money to continue our journey. From our farm we brought with us our cotton sacks; so we got a job on a farm, and we all went picking cotton, from my little sister, who was four, and on up to the oldest sister. Since 1929 had been so dry, the cotton stalks were about two to three feet high. Some of the bolls were so small and tightly closed the farmer let us strip it. We would start at the bottom of the stalk and interlace our fingers. Then we would pull up and strip everything from the stalk – bolls, leaves, et cetera. I believe at that time we were paid $.75 per hundredweight. All of the family together could pick approximately 2,000 pounds. This would give us approximately $15.00 for our day's work. After a week or two picking cotton, we were on our trip again to California.

Continuing our journey, we entered Arizona where we ran short of money again; so we stopped to pick some more cotton. Instead of cotton like in Texas, this was another variety called "pima." It was a high-grade cotton and couldn't be stripped but had to be picked out of the boll. One of the drawbacks to picking the pima cotton was their small bolls which had only three small locks of cotton in them. You couldn't use gloves to pick, and the sharp burrs just tore up the cuticles on one's fingers. By the day's end, our fingers were bleeding. To keep from having our fingers cut up, we would wrap a small band of adhesive tape around the finger completely over the cuticle. This was of great help, but another problem for us small children was the very rank cotton. We would have to push or bulldoze our way through the tangled mess.

My poor mother after a hard day of picking cotton would have to patch some of our cotton sacks. The bottoms of the sacks, as we pulled them across the bare ground, wore out fairly often. My mother would have to work by a kerosene lantern into the night to repair them. A lot of the farmers raising cotton sometimes didn't make enough to cover the cost of picking, ginning, and raising the crop, the reason being that the boll weevil destroyed a lot of the cotton crops in Texas and Arizona. In the weeks it took us to travel through Texas and Arizona, we never had money for a motel or one of the small cabins along the way. We simply made camp by the edge of the highway or in a field and cooked and slept in the open.

When we entered the state of California, the word was oranges could be picked right off the trees, and work was plentiful. We were stopped at the border by the border guards. They asked us where we were from and what states we had come through. My dad told them, and the guards said to protect California from the boll weevil, we had to boil all of our blankets, cotton sacks, bed ticking, et cetera, before we could cross the border. They had huge pots of boiling water, and we had to put all of our clothing, bedding, et cetera, in the pots and wash them. After washing we had to hang them on lines to dry. This took us two or three days to complete. Then we were allowed into California.

Brawley, CA, in 1929 where we picked dates. Posing in front of date tree, from left to right, are sisters Ruby, Ethel, and Vivian.)

We were again getting a little short of money; so not very far from the border was a small town called Brawley. We made camp beside the road and in a clearing of mesquite bushes. The next day my dad went looking for work and came back, telling us he had found a job for us picking dates. The orchard was watered via irrigation ditches. My brother Milburn, who was about two years old at the time, fell into one of the ditches. My oldest sister, Ethel, saw my brother trying to rise up out of the water unsuccessfully; so she had to rescue him or he would have drowned.

My mother with daughter Lillian and son Milburn in date orchard, 1929.)

After a couple weeks, we made enough money to continue on. We landed outside a small town called "Wasco." My father soon got a job with a farmer, Mr. Frantz, helping him with plowing and planting his crops. Mr. Frantz had no house we could stay in, but on part of the property was a huge Eucalyptus tree grove where he let us camp, and we pitched our tent. My mother with sheets, blanket, and rope enclosed the area so no one could see us. Later Mr. Frantz let us clean out an old cow barn where we stayed for some time.

My father worked for Mr. Frantz, and mother worked chopping cotton or cutting potatoes for spring planting. Cutting potatoes with a big butcher knife is quite a science as you have to cut each piece so it has an eye in it. If a piece had no eye, no plant would come up. On weekends, us kids would help our mother chop cotton, or weed cotton, also prune grapes and tie them up. I think the hourly rate at that time was approximately $.25 per hour. In the summertime we worked the whole week picking cotton, picking potatoes, or cutting grapes. We were always glad when school began as we had only to work on weekends.

I can remember in the summertime working all week in the fields. On Saturday night we would all take a bath and go with mom and dad into town. Mom and dad would shop for groceries for the coming week. For all our labor, our dad would give us each $.25 to spend as we pleased. You could go to the movies for $.10. Cokes, candy bars, and a bag of popcorn cost $.05 each. We were in seventh heaven.

We rode the bus to school until we moved to town. In town you had to walk to school no matter if it was eight or ten blocks. The busses were for the children who lived out in the country.

Home at 1922 Fourth Street, Wasco, California, in 1941. From left to right, sisters Ruby, Vivian, and Ethel; our mother; Alan Amos; myself; sisters Lillian and Viola.)

Dad found a house in the town of Wasco and traded his $500 car for the property, and that was where we resided the greater part of our life. The city of Wasco at that time had no sewer system, and we had the usual two- or three-holer in the backyard; however, it wasn't long before they had a sewer system, and we added a bathroom to our house. This house was about a block north of the Wasco Union High school campus, and later I will tell you of the fun times my little friends and I had on campus.

When we moved to town, my dad made little rabbit hutches where he raised tame rabbits to eat. I would watch, and it was like in Oklahoma – he would take a rabbit out of the cage, hold it up by its hind feet, and bring the edge of his other hand hard down behind the rabbit's head. Then he would have me hold the rabbit's hind legs, and with his knife he would make a few cuts and then pull the complete skin off the rabbit.

We also grew baby chicks for frying chickens in the backyard. One day my mother while doing dishes looked out the kitchen window and saw a cat amongst our baby chickens. She said to my dad, "Oscar, there's a cat out there eating our baby chickens." My father went into his bedroom, got his double-barreled shotgun, and came back into the kitchen. He quietly opened the back door and with his foot kicked open the screen door. The cat started up over the fence, and my father let go with a shot. The cat went head over heels and was dead. The pellets from the shot peppered the house across the alley like hail. Hearing this, the neighbors started coming out of their back doors, but when they saw who had shot the gun, they retreated into their houses. My dad could be a real mean individual, and the neighbors knew it.

For example, when I was in the fourth grade, a larger boy chased me home. I opened the front gate, ran up the walk to the front porch, and as I was about to open the front door, my dad opened it and said, "What is the matter?" I said, "The boy out front wants to beat me up." He said, "Do you want me to spank you with my razor strop, or do you want to fight that boy?" I knew from previous spankings how they hurt, and I went out and fought the boy. It was about an even fight. I bloodied his nose and he bloodied mine. As I went back through the gate and up the steps, my father said, "That's better." He said, "Don't ever run from anyone. If they are bigger than you are, pick up a rock or 2 x 4 and hit them in the head."

Another example of how mean he was concerned my five sisters. After each meal he would say, "Ruby, you wash the dishes, and, Vivian, you dry them." Sometimes if they had just done the dishes from the previous meal, Ruby would say to him, "Why can't Lillian or Ethel do them?" This would make my dad so angry that with his open palm he would knock Ruby clear across the room. It was my and my little brother, Milburn's, job to take all the leaves in the yard and to mow the lawn every Saturday and Sunday. Our daddy didn't tell us to do this as we knew what he would do to us if we didn't rake the leaves and mow the lawn.

My father, center, with two buddies in France during WWI, garbed in WWI uniforms.)

My father served in the army during WWI. The picture above shows him with two of his army buddies. I have a memento of my father's service in WWI. It is his water canteen which he carried. On the boat trip back to the United States, a black buddy of his took his pocket knife and etched an elaborate design of flowers and trees on it. In a square he also carved the wording, "Argonne Woods, September 18, 1918."

Oscar, my father, with friend in Paris, France, during WWI.)

In 1935 my father died at the age of 40 from a disease called "Tularemia," or rabbit fever. The doctor said he either got scratched by a rabbit or got scratched by the wire pen when he reached in to take out a rabbit. At that time there was no known cure, and he died within three or four days.

My five sisters. From left to right, Ethel, Viola, Lillian, Vivian, and Ruby.)

When dad died, the children were as follows: Milburn, 7; Lillian, 9; Vivian, 13; Ruby, 15; Ethel, 18; Viola, 20;

and myself, 11. By this time Ethel and Viola had married. Mother, because my dad had served in the army during the WWI, received a monthly check of $52.00 to feed and clothe five children still at home. My poor mother worked from daylight to dark in the fields so we could have food and some clothing. My mother was too proud to take any welfare. I remember when I was in the fourth and fifth grades, I would run home at 2:30 p.m. when school was dismissed and would change my clothes, get my cotton sack, and run to the end of the block where the city limits ended. Across the road was a cotton field, and I would help my mother pick cotton until it was almost dark. On Saturdays all of us children would go with mother and pick cotton. When your sack was full, you had to throw it over your shoulders and walk up to the scales at the wagon to weigh it. After it was weighed and the weigh master had put the pounds picked in his little book, then we climbed up a ladder and emptied our sacks into the wagon.

Sometimes the weigh master was real nice and would empty the sacks for the women; however, sometimes he would not. There were quite a few Negroes also in the fields picking cotton. They were the nicest and kindest in the world and would go out of their way to help you. As they picked cotton, they would sing songs which were mostly spiritual. The one song I loved to hear them sing was, <u>Ole Man River</u>. Even today I know all the words by heart.

My sister, Ruby, was a good cotton picker, and I always liked to pick a row beside her. One day when I was about 14 years old and we started picking cotton, I said to her that I bet I can beat you. We picked like mad all day long, but while I picked a little over 400 pounds, she had picked almost 500 pounds.

Years later she said I was fast but the reason she could beat me was because I had so much lost motion. She went on to say, "You pick four or five bolls and then put them in your sack. You see, I pick 10 or 12 bolls before I put them in my sack." Once in while we would put an unopened boll in our sack to get a little extra weight.

Before cotton-picking time, there was potato-picking time. A tractor pulled the potato digger. The digger had a sharp front like a plow which would lift the potatoes up out of the ground and onto a big metal chain conveyor belt. The conveyor would drop the potatoes on the ground, and you would pick them up in a gunnysack. You had to put at least 50 pounds in each sack for which you were paid $.05 per sack.

This was in the summer, and temperature would reach 105 to 120 degrees with no shade whatsoever. Sometimes if the car was close, we'd sit in the shade of it for a minute or so before the tractor came around again.

Around your waist you wore a large, broad belt onto which a piece of heavy wire or big nail was bent into a U shape. These hooks were at the front of the belt approximately 12" to 16" apart, and on these hooks you hung seven or eight empty gunnysacks. These you slung between your legs while you bent over face down picking up potatoes to put in the sacks. When you got about 50 pounds in the sack, you would lift it off the hooks, step aside, and set the bag in line with the bags previously picked. We worked from 7:00 a.m. to 12:00 noon. Then from 1:00 p.m. to 5:00 or 6:00 p.m. we would pick 100 sacks more or less which gave us $5.00 for a day's work.

Another job we had was cutting grapes for raisins. You would buy a big knife with a big curved blade, something like what they call a "linoleum knife" today, to cut the grapes. We would take a furnished wooden lug box and duck under the grapevines and cut the grapes into the lug box. When the box was full, you placed the grapes on a wooden 2'x 3' tray and spread the grapes on the tray to dry.

This was a dirty and dusty job, and one thing I didn't like most of all was the wasps' nests. To get rid of the wasps, we took a rolled-up newspaper and set fire to it, holding it under the wasp nest until they were killed. Sometimes one or two wasps stung you, and they really hurt. I had one of my eyes go shut when a wasp stung me just above my eyebrow. We were paid $.05 per tray, and if you were a good grape-cutter, you could make $5.00 to $6.00 per day. These days, all the above jobs are done by mechanical harvesters, but back then we did not need any illegal immigrants to do the above work. Mostly whites, Negroes, and a few Mexicans did the harvesting then. As I look back, all the heat, dust, and dirt did not seem to bother us. All of us have lived to the age of 70 or older.

Well, in growing up, boys will be boys and girls will be girls. My mother when we were not working would let us go to the Saturday afternoon matinee at the theater. You could get in for $.10 if you were 10 years old or younger, and even above this age, we would crouch down at the cashier's window and still get in for $.10. The Saturday afternoon matinee would run until 4:30 or 5:00 p.m. at which time they would empty the theater and close it until the evening showing at 7:00 p.m. When emptying the theater, my friends, Barney and Eddie, and I would hide under the seats until everyone was out and they had locked up. We would play all over the theater until someone came in to start the evening show at 7:00 p.m. We would sneak up into the loges to watch the same show we had seen that afternoon. We were big shots then because the loges were $.50 and not $.10 like the general admission.

My mother would not let us go to the movies on weekday nights as we had to study and get our rest. Barney's dad made good money, and sometimes he would give Barney $5.00 to go to the store to get some bread or milk. When Barney would get back home, he would give his dad back the change minus $.50 or $1.00.

Barney would come to my house and say, "Vernon, let's go to the movies tonight." I would ask my mother for her permission, and she'd say, "No. I don't have the money." I would say, "Barney is paying my way," and she would relent. My little sister, Lillian who was two years younger, would say, "Mom, why can't I go? You let Vernon go," and would start crying. Mother would again relent and give her $.10. Mother would say, "Vernon, you take your little sister with you or you cannot go." I would say, "Okay." And we would walk out of the house. Once outside I would say to my little sister, "You can come with us, but you have to walk behind us."

About this time we became fascinated with cards. We learned Spit in the Ocean, Pairs, and Poker. Another card game we learned was Rook. Barney's dad had bought a deck and taught us three boys how to play. Rook had four suits of cards just like regular cards only the suits were colored, i.e., red, black, green, and yellow.

Eddie and I would team up against Barney and another friend we had. Eddie and I devised signals beforehand. He had black hair, and if he had good cards in the black suit, he would run his fingers through his hair. I had a red ring, and if I had a good hand in that suit, I would rub the red ring. If he had good cards in the green suit, he would say something like, "I have to mow the grass tomorrow." Partners were determined by the cut of the cards, i.e., you'd pick a card before the start of the game, and the one with the highest card got to pick his partner. We played this game often;

however, we would sometimes play poker with chips. We learned this game by watching the players around the tables in the local saloons. At that time there was only a constable in town, and minors being in places they should not have been usually was not enforced.

About this time we boys became interested in the opposite sex. My sister had a girlfriend, and sometimes with my mother gone, we would let them play poker with us. My mother was very strict and would not let us play cards when she was home.

1942. In the Navy. Home on leave with friend, Ercell Pollard.)

A refreshment wagon was parked on the high school grounds. The students at the various athletic games would use it to sell cokes, candy, et cetera. When this wagon was not in use, it was parked in a big vacant area at the school. The wagon was never locked; so we boys would sneak into it and sit on the floor and play cards. One day we were in the wagon when my sister and her friend came by. We asked them to come in and play cards with us. We decided we would play strip poker, i.e., the person who got the highest card got to pick something to take off that others were wearing. Of course, we boys cheated a little, and pretty soon my sister's friend had nothing left on but her blouse and panties.

Eddie, our lookout, peeked out and noticed a custodian coming our way. We quickly gathered up our clothes, putting some on, while running for our lives.

As I said before, the law was a little lax, and we would go into the T & B saloon and watch the adult men play poker or watch them play pool. The T & B had three pool tables, and we noted that one table was very seldom used. We asked the manager if we could play pool on this table and he said, "Okay," but admonished us to take care of the pool sticks and the table. We boys played for a number of days on the pool table and afterwards would walk home. Well, one day as we were walking home, Barney pulled out of his jacket pocket a No. 8 pool ball. Eddie and I said, "Why did you take it and what are you going to do with it?" Barney said, "I am going to cut it in half to see if the number "8" runs completely through the ball." If you have ever played pool, you know that the number 8 appears to be in precisely the same location on opposite sides of the ball. When we got home, Barney got a hammer and a hatchet. He put the sharp edge of the hatchet on the ball and hit the peen end of the hatchet real hard with the hammer. Well, he cleaved the ball in two, and the inside was only solid black Bakelite.

As I said, we boys liked to play Rook over at Barney's house. One night a few days after the pool ball episode we were at Barney's and there came a knock at the door. Barney's dad, Tim, went to the door and opened it. Mr. Bernard said, "Hello, Lee. What can I do for you?" Lee, being Mr. Tribble, the town constable, said, "Would Barney be around?" Mr. Bernard said, "Yes. He and some of his friends are here playing Rook; so come on in."

Mr. Tribble said, "Barney, you and the boys were down at the T & B playing pool two or three days ago and they are missing the 8 ball. Do any of you know anything about it?" Barney spoke up and said, "Yes, I do." Mr. Tribble said, "You do? Do you know what happened to it?" Barney said, "I took it," and Mr. Tribble said, "You took it? Where is it?" And Barney said, "In my room."

Mr. Tribble said, "Would you go and get it." Barney went in his room, got the two halves of the 8 ball, and put them together like it was a whole ball. He came back into the front room where Mr. Tribble held out the palm of his hand for the ball. When Barney put the ball in Mr. Tribble's palm, it flopped apart. Mr. Tribble, shocked, exclaimed, "What happened to it?" Barney said, "I cut it in two to see if the "8" ran from one side of the ball to the other side." Mr. Tribble said, "Barney, you will have to pay for it," and Barney's dad said, "It's okay, Lee. We will take care of it."

Several days later Mr. Tribble came by and told Mr. Bernard the cost was $5.00 which he paid. After that, we were personas non grata at the T & B saloon.

Soon after this the telephone company decided to install telephone service to our part of the town. We boys were always going up and down the alleys to pick up bottles, copper wire, lead, et cetera, which we could sell to the junk man. Going down our alley, we found a piece of telephone cable three feet in length. This piece of cable had a lead sheath around it. The sheath wasn't very thick; so we stripped it off the copper wire. We then noticed the lead was about as thick as a nickel coin. We got a short piece of three-quarter-inch galvanized pipe and sharpened it on one end. After flattening the lead piece with a hammer on the sidewalk, we would take the sharpened pipe, place it on the lead, and hit it hard with a hammer. Voila! We had a coin the size of a nickel; however, it had sharp edges and burrs; so we rustled up two files, and while one would pound out the coins, the other two would file off the edges and burrs. When we finished, each of us had both pockets full of fake nickels.

We went downtown to a coke machine, put in a nickel slug, and got a coke. We would go to a candy bar machine and do the same. Boy, in a way we were rich, but we couldn't get in the movies with nickel slugs. You had to have real money. The three of us hitchhiked a ride to the neighboring town of Shafter, a distance of eight miles. Finally after hitting a number of coke and candy machines, we came to a small Chinese restaurant inside which was a mechanical horseracing machine similar to a slot machine. We had played a few slot machines and made a little money, but this horseracing machine had seven slots for the seven horses that raced. At the top of the machine where you'd put your nickel in for your horse was a lever that you'd pull to start the race. Sometimes you won, but mostly you lost. We noticed that when you put your nickel in a slot and pulled the lever, the finger on that lever would make contact with your nickel and start your horse. We said, "Why don't we put seven slugs in," as we were sure to get $.15 or more each time.

Boy, we were doing well. We would take the slugs out of one pocket and put the real money in the other pocket. One time I pulled the lever to make the little finger thing contact the slug and start the race. Well, there was a flaw in the slug as it was too thin and the finger went through it and would not release when we let go of the lever. The machine started going wild, and pretty soon it began to smoke. We ran out of there and went back to Wasco as soon as we could catch a ride. Once in Wasco, we could go to the show or buy anything as we had lots of real coins in our pockets.

In our little town was a combination bakery and soda fountain where all the kids congregated. They made good doughnuts at $.05 each, and you could buy a malt or a sundae at the fountain. About this time pinball machines came into being, and the bakery installed one over against a wall. Well, they were like a slot machine, and to play you had to put in a nickel. If by chance you won, the machine would show the number of games, and the fountain girl would pay you $.05 for each game the machine registered.

When you put your nickel in the machine, it gave you five steel balls. When you would shoot a ball, it rolled from top to bottom and would give you a certain score as it hit various coil-like bumpers on the way down. We'd always try to hit the bumpers that gave you the most points. When you exceeded the set amount of points, you won $.05 for each game you amassed over that amount. You could try to jiggle the machine to hit certain bumpers, but if you jiggled too much, the machine would say, "Tilt," and you would lose your nickel.

We noticed that way down on the machine were the bumpers which, when hit by the ball, scored the most. Since these bumpers were near the sides, we "appropriated" a small drill bit at school and drilled a small hole in the side of the machine opposite these bumpers. While Barney played the machine, Eddie would stand close to him on one side and I, on the other side. Eddie or I would insert a straightened-out paper clip in the hole and make contact with the bumpers which would record the score. As Barney played, we would keep watch but would jiggle on the clip as fast as we could. We would run up to 60 or 70 games and call the fountain girl over to verify the amount for us to collect our money. When she saw the number of games, she couldn't believe her eyes. When she paid us and we started to leave, she put a sign on the machine saying, "Out of Order." But a day or so later, we would come back in and do the same thing over. She would say to us, "I don't know how you can win so many games as others seldom win."

Another time we entered a small restaurant and they had a real old pinball machine. Instead of bumpers, it had rollovers, i.e., if you rolled over a pin sticking up, you got a certain score. Usually the machine was on such a slant that you couldn't jiggle it to make contact as the ball raced to the bottom and out of play. Barney, however, lifted the legs of the machine at the bottom and put them on the toes of his shoes. When the ball was shot, the slant of the machine was almost nil. He got the ball on a 1,000-score pin where it became stuck. Barney would lightly bump the machine with his hand, and the ball would go up and back again on the pin for another 1,000 score. Barney kept doing this until he had 99 games recorded on the machine and it would record no more. We called the owner over to check us out, and he too couldn't believe his eyes. He didn't have that much money -- $4.95 – in his cash register and had to give us a check. Subsequent to this, the makers of the pinball machines got wise to the faults of their machines and payouts were rendered scarce; so we finally quit playing them.

One day when Eddie, Barney, and I were walking home from school, we stopped to watch a fellow welding on a trailer. We were in the fifth grade at that time and had never seen any welding. We noticed the man had two large steel cylinder tanks on which were some gauges and some rubber hoses which ran to the torch he was using to weld two pieces of iron together. We asked him what was in the two big tanks that made the flame so hot that it welded the two pieces of iron together. He said one tank contained oxygen and the other contained carbide gas.

Close by were three or four five-gallon cans labeled "Union Carbide" on the side. About this time he said, "Oops. I am out of gas." He unscrewed the hoses and gauges from the top of the cylinder and twisted the top off. He filled a gallon bucket with carbide and put it in this cylinder. He then got a quart of water and also put this in the cylinder. Boy! He moved fast to screw the cap on the cylinder and hook up his gauges and hoses.

He said, "Let me show you what this carbide will do." He then got a one-pound coffee can, punched a nail hole in the bottom, and set it on a brick at an angle. He then put a few grains of carbide in the can and got some water and likewise put it in the can. He quickly put on the lid, stepped back, took a match, lit it, and held it to the nail hole. Boy, the lid blew off like a cannon and went flying across the street. We were in awe as to what a few grains of carbide could do.

He was a nice man and let us each take turns firing off the cannon. We thanked him and went on our way home.

Two or three weeks later was the Fourth of July. We had no money for fireworks and were at a loss as to what we could do. Barney happened to think of the "carbide man." So late that night we all three went down the alley to where the carbide was. Barney and I held the fence up while Eddie crawled under. Eddie pried the lid off one of the cans and filled his pockets with carbide. He crawled back under the fence and we boys flew down the alley as dogs started to bark.

Well, the Fourth of July came and we were in Barney's backyard. We had our one-pound coffee can all set up. As it began to get dark, we lit off a charge. Boy, it was loud and some of the neighbors came out of their houses to see what was going on.

After a few shots with the one-pound can, we found a three-pound coffee can. We fixed it up and loaded it with a little more carbide and water than we had with the one-pound can. Boy, when Eddie lit a match to the nail hole, it went off louder than a canon and it really shook the neighborhood up.

A little later Eddie said, "My mom has an empty five-gallon lard can at home, and I will go and get it." When he got back, we fixed it up like the previous cans. Eddie said, "Since it's a bigger can, let's put in a cup of carbide and a cup of water." Eddie did this, put the lid on, and tried to light a match to put at the nail hole. The first match wouldn't light and neither would the second match. By the time he got a third match to light, a good minute had elapsed. When he finally did touch the hole with the match, not only did it blow the lid approximately 100 feet away but it blew the whole five-gallon can apart.

The neighbors got so angry they said they were going to call the police. We gathered our stuff up and went to the end of our street which was the west boundary of the city. In the open field across the street, we fired our one-pound and three-pound coffee can bombs until we were out of carbide.

All in all, it was a good Fourth of July 'cuz we were not killed when our five-gallon bomb blew apart.

Finally the day came when I entered high school. My days of crawling under the fence to see the football games and track meets were over. No more swiping loquats and walking around the ledge of the auditorium. I had only been a freshman for four or five days when the head custodian, Mr. Unruh, stopped me and said he would like to see me after school. I expected the worst for the hard times we boys had given the custodians. I met Mr. Unruh after school, and he asked me if I would like to work part-time for him. He said he needed four boys to work after school cleaning the blackboards, sweeping floors, and washing windows. He also said he needed a boy to help the gardener mow the lawns, trim hedges, and plant flowers. I liked being outside; so I opted to be the gardener's helper. I would work from 6:00 a.m. to 8:00 a.m. then go to school until 4:00 p.m. Then I would resume work from 4:00 p.m. to 6:00 p.m. On Saturdays we worked from 8:00 a.m. to 12:00 noon. I was paid $.75 per hour which gave me $18.00 per week. This work helped me to purchase my clothes and have a little spending money.

This program was called the National Youth Authority and was designated to help those boys who came from poor families. It was a good program, and it sure helped me. My little brother, Milburn, who was four years younger than I also worked four years at high school doing janitorial work.

One benefit about being a custodian's helper was you became acquainted with almost all of the teachers. In my freshman year, I had to take English as one of my required subjects. Ms. Beatrice Casey was my teacher and just out of college. She was a little on the heavy side but very cute and very endowed top side. The school was getting a little crowded and schoolrooms were at a premium; so our class was held in the band room at the rear of the auditorium. One day Ms. Casey who had her back to us while putting something on the blackboard was shot in her posterior by a boy in the class armed with a big rubber band and some real wire staples. I knew it hurt really bad as tears came into her eyes. Another boy, Lee, and I got up from our desks, grabbed the boy, and started to throw him out of the window. Ms. Casey said, "Vernon and Lee, let him be as I will take care of him." We never did see the boy in class again.

Another class everyone was required to take and pass before you could receive your diploma was U.S. History. The class was taught by Ms. Buckingham. She had taught this class for years and did not tolerate any nonsense. My buddy, Lee, and I were the only two boys in a class of all girls. Lee and I would go to study hall early in the morning and bone up on the history lesson for that day. Close to the end of class period, Ms. Buckingham would start to ask questions on the lesson she had given the day before. Lee and I would raise our hands, and she would call on one of us to give the answer, which we did. She would ask another question, and we would raise our hands again. Finally, Ms. Buckingham said, "Vernon and Lee, keep your hands down and let some of the girls answer the questions."

Lee and I would not study for the next day's lesson, but when it came time to answer the questions, we would raise our hands. Ms. Buckingham would say, "Vernon and Lee, keep your hands down. You answered all the questions yesterday. Let the girls answer them now." One day Ms. Buckingham said, "Vernon and Lee, I want to see you after school." "What did we do?" We asked, "Haven't we been doing good in class?" She said, "You have been doing good, but I want to talk to you after school as I have no time now." Well, we went to see her after school, and she said, "Vernon and Lee, you would be straight-A students if you would do a little outlining of my lessons at night." She said, "For class participation I can only give you a B grade." We said, "That's okay with us," and she excused us with a smile on her face.

Prior to being a junior, I would hear other students taking Ms. Buckingham's class say, "That old so-and-so flunked me or gave me a D grade," but to Lee and me, she was a stern but good teacher.

The high school did not have a cafeteria then. We either carried our lunch, went home for it, or went downtown to the drive-in called "Beaner's." This was a hangout for kids who wanted a coke, hamburger, fries, et cetera. Some of the students had automobiles; so when the noon bell rang, it was a race to get in your car and be the first to go to Beaner's and place your order.

There were two brothers by the name of Perkins who had an old car whose exhaust smoked like a diesel truck. Instead of buying good oil for their engine, they would use drain oil from other cars. I guess this was the reason their car smoked like it did. Anyway, these two boys would back their car into a space in the parking lot to make a fast get-away at lunch. Around the parking lot was a low four-inch steel-pipe railing attached to vertical steel posts which were embedded in cement. One day another student brought to school in his car an approximate 30-foot length of heavy log chain. He wrapped one end of the chain around the railing and the other end around the rear transmission of the Perkins' car.

The noon bell rang, and the kids with cars raced to get in them. The Perkins brothers jumped in their car and gave it the gas. Well, when they reached the end of the chain tied to the car and the steel posts, the force pulled the whole rear end, tires and all, out from under the car. Some of us who were in on the joke laughed so hard we almost cried.

I was a senior in 1942. With the war going on, a lot of my friends were enlisting in the various services. I wanted to join the navy, but being 17, I could not. If you were under the age of 18, you had to have your parents' consent to enlist. After several weeks of pleading with my mother, she finally agreed to sign so I could join the navy.

Upon finishing boot camp, Bill Boyce, a new friend I'd met, and I put in for electrician school. We were assigned to a class of 150 men at the Electrical Engineering School of the University of Minnesota.

Upon finishing this seven-month class and receiving our third class petty officer rating, we put in for another school. We were assigned to the Motion Picture Technician School at the Naval Training Base at San Diego. This was a three-month course, teaching the operation and maintenance of 16mm and 35mm projectors and their sound systems.

During my boot training and the electrical training, I never did receive home leave. At the San Diego school, you were permitted a weekend leave at least every other week depending on which side you were stationed, i.e., portside or starboard side. I was on the portside whereas my friend, Bill, was on the starboard side. Since Bill was from New York, he just elected to stay on base and would give me his pass so I could go home to Wasco almost every weekend.

After this school, I was ordered to the 13th Naval District Headquarters at Seattle, Washington, where I was assigned to the Training Aids Division.

Here we issued training films to the various ships and bases in our area. I also taught the operation of 16mm and 35mm projectors to classes of approximately 35 men from the different ships which came into Port of Seattle. We also had a small auditorium where we would show films to the different naval departments as requested, these departments being medical, gunnery, et cetera.

After 21 months with the training aids division, I was assigned to the training station at Bremerton, Washington. After waiting approximately two months at Bremerton, I caught the aircraft carrier CVE 97 USS Thetis Bay where I was assigned to the Electrical Division on the ship.

My duties as electrician on the ship were varied, but the most important thing was being assigned as the ship's motion picture operator. Every night on the hangar deck from a booth suspended under the flight deck, I would show movies to the various crewmembers, including the captain.

Every afternoon as I was inspecting the film for that night's showing, I would get a visit from the captain's chief master at arms. He would say, "Sparks, what are we showing tonight?" And I would tell him. He would say, "That sounds like a good one, and I will tell the captain." Then he would tell me, "Now, don't start until the Captain comes down the gangway and sits down. If the Captain isn't coming down, I will come down the gangway and give you the signal to start."

Sometimes we were six months at sea without seeing land. Since we had approximately 15 movies onboard, we would trade off with the other carriers in our fleet; a destroyer assigned to our fleet would take movies from one carrier to another carrier and vice versa.

At no time in the battle zone were carriers allowed to stop for anything, no matter how serious. Our destroyer escorts were very helpful in this regard. Sometimes when one of our airplanes became so shot up in battle that it was unable to land on our flight deck and had to be ditched at sea, the destroyer would pick up the pilot and gunner of the crippled plane and return them to our ship.

Onboard ship we made our own ice cream day in and day out for our crew. Sometimes as a destroyer would return our fliers to us, we would reward them with 25 to 30 gallons of ice cream, our terms being, "Please return our ice cream containers to us."

It was very hot out in the Pacific both day and night. After morning muster, Bill and I, now second-grade petty officers, would assign the six or seven men under our command their duties for the day. As soon as this was done, Bill and I would go down to the after mess hall to the "Geedunk" stand. There they sold razors, shaving cream, candy bars, cigarettes, et cetera. They also made the best ice cream sundaes; so Bill and I would get one and go over and sit down with our backs to the bulkhead. Soon we would be joined by one of our men and then another and then another until all of our crew was there. We would sit there for 20 or 30 minutes eating our ice cream and then we would say, "Okay, boys. It's time to go to work."

During the war, you could buy cigarettes for $.05 a pack, or $.45 a carton. There were Camels, Lucky Strikes, Chesterfields, and Pall Malls. I smoked Pall Malls and a fellow by the name of Maloney in our division smoked Camels. Camels were always at a premium, and if you couldn't get these, you smoked another brand. One day I was at the "Geedunk" stand when they opened a big case of Camels. I told the storekeeper I wanted five cartons, but he said, "Sorry, Sparks. Only two to a customer." I took my two cartons, one under each arm, and went down to our compartment. Maloney saw them and said, "Where did you get them?" I told him, "At the 'Geedunk' stand," and out he rushed and up the ladder. Pretty soon he returned and said they had sold out before he could get there. He bartered two cartons of Chesterfields for one carton of Camels. To make a story short, I didn't like Camels but finally got seven cartons of Chesterfields for one carton of Camels.

Smoking onboard ship was only allowed on the flight deck, outer sponsons, fantail, and bow. Sometimes when fueling aircraft or loading ammo or fuel, you would hear the loudspeaker say, "Now hear this: The smoking lamp is out throughout the ship." Only when they would announce the smoking lamp was lit could you smoke again.

My ship saw action in the battles of Saipan, Iwo Jima, and Okinawa. Being with the big battle group Halsey's Third

Fleet, we feared mostly submarines and kamikaze pilots. During battle the carrier stood well out of range of land-based artillery, deploying our planes to do the damage. We were never hit and suffered no casualties.

No matter if you had "turned to," meaning went to work, during the day, you had to stand your four-hour watch at night. Sleep was at a premium. My four-hour watch was also down in the electrician shop where you were on call to make repairs anywhere on the ship.

On one occasion a big electric motor on one of the two large freezer compressors burned up. If the other motor went out, all the perishables on the ship would have spoiled. Bill and I had to take the big electric motor off the compressor and up to the electric shop to rewind it. Then we had to take it back down to the after-engine room and install it. We had to work over 24 hours steady to do this, and with no air conditioning in the after-engine room, it became an oven. My clothes were completely soaked with sweat, and later on when I opened my wallet, all the paper money had mildewed.

During my stay in Seattle, I went to a roller-skating rink one night. I could not skate too well, but when it was ladies' choice, this young girl came over and asked me to skate. Her name was Mary, and I saw her several times before I was shipped out. She wrote me often, and I did so in return.

When I got out of the Navy in November, 1945, I returned to Wasco, California, and started work as a meter-reader for the Pacific Gas & Electric Company. On January 19, 1946, I had hooked up with my friend Lee from high school days. He had a job tending bar downtown at one of the watering holes. It was pretty much party time most of the nights, but that grew pretty old. I had written Mary and told her I wanted to marry her, and she wrote me back saying she loved me. I did not know how I could get to Seattle as I had no car, because after the war, cars were scarce.

One Wednesday night, Lee and I were at this restaurant, and he had the next four days off. I told him I wanted to go to Seattle and get married. He said, "Let's go" -- He had a Ford coupe – and I said, "When?" He said, "Right now." I said, "Let's wait until tomorrow and drive to Seattle (1,000 miles) on Thursday and Friday. Then I will get married, and we can drive back home on Saturday and Sunday and be at work on Monday." Well, Mary didn't want a quickie marriage and neither did her friends and family. We were granted a license with a time-waiver exception and were married in the church within three days. I had not notified my boss yet of my absence; so I didn't know if I would still have a job when I got home. If I had no job, I would stay in Seattle and find one. I sent a telegram to my boss saying, "Just got married. If I come back, can I have my old job back?" He sent a return telegram saying, "Come on back. Now that you are married, you may need the job."

My wife and I on our wedding day, May 30, 1946, in Seattle, Washington.)

After my marriage, we returned to Wasco and I resumed my job as meter-reader. We stayed at my mother's house for ten days then found a small apartment over a double garage. It was about three blocks from the center of town.

After the war, cars were hard to get, and you had to be on a waiting list for one. When we needed groceries, we had to walk to town and carry them back home. For entertainment we walked downtown to the movie theater once in a while.

For my duties as a meter-reader for PG & E, I was provided a car for my work. When we got a new local manager for our service area, he was a very kind person, and he permitted me to take my company car home at night. This was a blessing as I could take it to get groceries.

As I said, our local manager, Mr. Sirman, was real nice. One day I was reading the electric meters in town in an area close to a barbershop. I needed a haircut; so I went in and sat down to wait my turn. The barber had a customer in his chair that was reading a newspaper. Soon the barber had completed his job, and the customer lowered his newspaper and got out of the chair. I was surprised to see Mr. Sirman and didn't know what to do, but he said, "Vernon, it grows on company time; so why not get it cut on company time?"

Reading meters was a good job which paid approximately $60.00 a week. With my wife working as a checker at Safeway stores, we saved most of our money. In 1949, the Ford Mercury dealer called and said our name on his list for a new car had come up. We went in and bought a new 1949 Mercury sedan and paid approximately $2,585.00.

Our landlord lived in a two-bedroom home to the right of our apartment, and they owned a two-bedroom rental on our left. We got to know our landlord real well, and they liked us very much; so they let us rent the two-bedroom house when it became empty.

At about this time, my wife got pregnant, and we had our first child, a son. Talking about new parents, we would get up every hour on the hour at night to see if the house temperature was 70 degrees. My new son had the colic and woke up every hour on the hour and my wife and me with him. After a few sleepless nights, I told my wife I had to go to work. Since she no longer worked, she could sleep and wake when he did. With this I went into the other bedroom and closed the door and went to sleep.

In 1950 we wanted a home of our own. House construction in Wasco was sporadic; so when they built a new subdivision of homes in Shafter, we bought one. It was a new 1,200 square foot three-bedroom home on a huge lot with a two-car garage. The price was $9,950 with $250 down. I got a veteran's loan at 3-3/4 % and my payments were $56.00 per month which included principal, interest, insurance, and property taxes.

Since I made approximately $60.00 per week and with all the new furniture we needed and the costs associated with the new baby, I didn't see how we could make it. For the first several months, we had to hang sheets on the windows as we could not afford blinds or drapes. I did all of the yard landscaping and tree planting. After approximately 23 years, we paid the house off. At the time of this writing, it is worth approximately $260,000.

Our next child born in 1952 was a girl we named Nancy, and after that, in 1955, came our second daughter, Paula. All of the new houses on our block were bought mostly by newlyweds; so in a few years when the school bus stopped to pick up the children in our block, there were approximately 37 who caught the bus.

My wife, when the children were young and at school, got a part-time job in the Shafter High School cafeteria. This allowed her to see the children off to school and be there when they returned. My wife was a hard worker, and when the kids grew a little older, she was made cafeteria manager of the high school where she worked 27 years before retiring.

One day I was mowing the front lawn and my children plus six or eight neighbor children were playing in the yard. A pickup pulled up at the curb with the back end loaded with baby lambs. The man asked the children if they wanted a lamb for free. My children ran over to me and begged for a little lamb, and I agreed. The man said that the mother sheep who had multiple births would only take care of one and the others like in the back of the pickup would die.

About this time a new shampoo came out showing a little lamb dancing about. The lamb's name was Pamper, and that's what the children named their lamb. Being so young, the children had to feed him via a baby bottle. Later on as he grew bigger, he would eat almost everything including our flowers and shrubs. He was like a puppy with the children, following them wherever they went. They would take him and bathe him in our bathtub. Nearly a year old, he was eating everything in sight, and we had to get rid of him. The children cried; so we had to do something to ease their sorrow.

Son Vernon and daughter Nancy in our backyard in Shafter, CA, with Peter Cottontail, the family rabbit.)

My sister, Ruby, and her husband, Bill, lived on an oilfield lease out in the country; so we told the children we were taking Pamper to put in Uncle Bill's corral. Every now and then, we would go to see Aunt Ruby, Uncle Bill and Pamper. On one trip Pamper was gone and the children asked Uncle

Bill what happened to him. Uncle Bill said, "Pamper got out and I guess the coyotes got him." The meat we had for our dinner that night was delicious.

In 1957 the Forestry Service had opened up a subdivision of 41 lots on forestry land in the Sequoia National Forest. We applied for one which we received and started to build on. Year after year on weekends we would take our old pickup to the mountains and work on our home. After several years we completed it. Today it is a nice place to go to get out of the hustle and bustle of city life. The children had fun while the building was going on, and to this day my son goes up there whenever he can to fish for trout and hunt for mushrooms.

While building our summer home, the three children slept in their sleeping bags in a tent. My wife and I slept on a day bed out in the open under the big pine trees. We were really in the forest primeval and at night you could hear the deer or bear crashing through the underbrush on their way down the mountain to the river. We also ate our meals on a picnic table and benches which we brought from home. My wife did all the cooking on a small, two-burner Coleman camping stove.

Building our summer home at Camp Nelson, CA, in 1957. Left to right, Paula, 3; Nancy, 5; and Vernon, 7.)

Every afternoon my wife would take the children to a small stream called "Bear Creek." There she would strip them naked and bathe them in the cold water – and I do mean cold water. When I would take my bath, the water, which was snowmelt from higher elevations, would take my breath away.

One thing that happened still leaves us thinking that God was looking over us. I had the day before dug a trench from under the house to our septic tank located approximately seven feet away. I was going to lay the sewer pipe in this trench which you had to step over when going around the house. The ditch was approximately a foot wide and two feet deep and the children could step over it. Well, Paula, who was three, came around to the front of the house yelling, "Momma, Daddy, the snake in the ditch, he jump at me." I got my shovel and ran around the house to the ditch where a four-foot rattlesnake was coiled. I took my shovel and cut him in two. Just north of this location, I killed another rattlesnake which was evidently its mate. In our 40 years since, we have never seen another snake and neither have our neighbors. Thank God Paula was not bitten.

After getting all the underpinning, stem walls, roof sheeting and roofing up, we were ready to move in. Although the siding was not on, we were out of the rain with the roof on. Even my son Vernon learned how to drive nails into the sub flooring. The girls furnished me and the carpenter I hired with water and kept the wood scraps out of our way.

Life was going good for us. We lived in a nice neighborhood of new homes and the children were starting to school. Their teachers were real nice and taught the children reading, writing, and arithmetic. Below is a picture of my daughter Nancy, who was in kindergarten, together with her brother Vernon, who was in the first grade.

First day of school. Daughter Nancy and son Vernon waiting for on sidewalk in front of our residence for school bus.)

The picture isn't very clear, but if you will look, you will see Vernon is missing his two front teeth. The school had a swimming pool, and the kids loved to swim. There was a sign posted which said, "Please do not run." Of course, my son disregarded the sign and fell, breaking off two of his front teeth. When he came home, we met him at the door, and he said, "Look, Ma. No teeth," and opened his mouth wide.

All of our children graduated from high school in Shafter and have done well in life. Our son Vernon is an independent contractor. Our oldest daughter Nancy is Senior Manager, I.T. Contracts, for DirecTV at the El Segundo office in Los Angeles. Our youngest, Paula, is a court reporter for Los Angeles Superior Court at the Antelope Valley Courthouse.

Son Vernon at the San Diego Zoo, circa 1957.)

One day we took the children to the zoo in San Diego which the children really enjoyed. The picture above shows my son riding one of the big tortoises they had there. The children took turns riding them. All in all, my wife and I have enjoyed our marriage as attested by the picture below which was taken on our 50th wedding anniversary. As of this writing we have been married over 61 years. The Lord has blessed us and our children.

From left to right, mother's sisters Mattie, Sarah, and Ocie; my mother.)

In closing, I wish to give honor to my mother. It was she, after our father died, who was the sole support of all of us children. She worked in the fields chopping cotton, picking cotton, cutting potatoes, picking potatoes, and cutting grapes for raisins. She worked from sun up to sundown six to seven days a week.

We always had food on the table although supper sometimes consisted only of a glass of buttermilk and a piece of cornbread. We always had fresh laundered clothes even though they had patches on them from being worn so much.

The whole family, mother excepted. From left to right, sister Ruby; brother-in-law John Lewis; sister Lillian; myself; my wife Mary; sister Ethel; brother-in-law Tom Settlemire; sister-in-law Jane; brother Milburn; sisters Viola and Vivian.)

Mary and Vernon on our fiftieth wedding anniversary, 1996.)

Mr. Lawson was born in April, 1924, in Porum, Oklahoma, the fifth child in a family of seven children. From the Dust

Bowl in 1929, his family moved to Wasco, California, where he received his education through high school.

In November, 1942, he joined the U.S. Navy, serving for over three years, and ended his naval career as an electrician aboard a CVE, aka baby flat top.

In May, 1946, he married his wife, Mary, the union resulting in three children.

I have led an interesting life as a supervisor for a public utility company, administrator for a domestic products company, independent businessman, and instructor for a trade school in the subjects of auto body repair and carpentry.

The Lawsons are now retired and after 61 years of marriage enjoy time together gardening and traveling.

NOTES (See Page 25.)

1. The history of Wasco dates back to 1897 when the Santa Fe Railroad laid tracks through the town. During the next several years, over 300 families relocated to the area primarily through arrangements made by Marshall V. Hartranft. Hartranft secured nine 640-acre sections from the Kern County Land Company for resale to those settlers, and he is therefore credited with inception of the new community. Hartranft's effort in bringing settlers to Wasco was titled the "Fourth Home Extension Colony."

   The town of Wasco was originally named "Dewey" and then "Deweyville." When William Bonham, a settler from Wasco County in Oregon, determined that there was a town already named "Deweyville," he proposed the area be renamed "Wasco," and in 1900 the Post Office recorded the town name of Wasco.

   There is scant agreement, however, among those who offer opinions as to the English translation of "wasco." Some say it means "hot," which would be appropriate given the climate of the region, but it may also mean "a large body of water" or even "a cup or small bowl made of bone."

By 1904, two schools united under the name, "Delta-Shamrock School." The Delta building served a multi-purpose function as the school and an educational/civic center for settlers who arrived in 1907. The school was eventually renamed "Wasco," and in 1919, when combined with the Elmo District, it became the Wasco School District.

Land was distributed to the new colonists on February 7, 1907. Wasco's business district consisted of a depot, general store, post office, two saloons, a blacksmith shop, and a hotel. Among settlers in the early 1900's was A.V. Bennet. He farmed alfalfa and launched a dairy business. Bennet subsequently introduced the area's first milk distribution service by delivering the bottled product to customers in Wasco and Lost Hills.

The Community's first church was organized in 1907, along with King Lumber Company and the Wasco Improvement Club. Among the Club's itinerary was the planting of shade trees and the purchase of firefighting equipment. Water was a primary concern and subsequently caused the development of the

Fourth Extension Water Company, an organization established to supply water for domestic and irrigation purposes.

Wasco nestles cozily among blooming rose fields, almond and pistachio orchards, sugar beets, grapes, many varieties of fruits and vegetables and white cotton fields. Wasco is universally known as the Rose Capital of the Nation. Strategically located in California's central valley, Wasco is the gateway to the central coast.

NOTES (See Page 55.)

1. In 1915, the voters of the Cleveland, Maple, Poplar, Wildwood, Semitropic, and Wasco elementary school districts approved the formation of a high school district for the community. Twenty-eight students were enrolled in Wasco High School that first year and classes were held in a rented auditorium-like building called "Wasco Hall."

A successful $45,000 bond election was held in December of 1915 and a portion of the funds thus generated was used to purchase a fifteen-acre school site at Trogdon's Corner. An adjacent three-acre parcel, labeled "Lot 48," of the Fourth Home Extension Colony was also purchased.

In August of 1916, the board accepted a bid of $44,552 for construction of the new high school building. It was completed in six months, and the cost at completion was about $50,000. Sixty-one students were enrolled at the time of the dedication on March 3, 1917. (The new high school building included both classrooms and the school offices and was in regular service until shortly before being razed in 1957.) After 1917, as new structures were added to the campus, this original building was referred to simply as the "Main Building."

NOTES (See Page 55.)

1. In the years following the opening of the Main Building, a host of new buildings were added to the campus: an industrial arts building in 1925, an auditorium in 1929, a gymnasium in 1931, an agricultural addition to the industrial arts building in 1934, the first phase of the science building in 1935, then the second phase in 1939. The cafeteria and a language arts building

were added in 1949, a library and a music building in 1953, a new classroom building and a bus garage in 1957, and a new administration building in 1959.

Although the renovation projects greatly altered the school's appearance, the old auditorium remains the centerpiece of the Wasco High School campus. Its unique architectural splendor has been beautifully preserved and, in 1998, it was placed on the National Register of Historic Places, 97001188. It seats 1200 and is still used for student assemblies, plays, musicals, et cetera. The fabric covering the seats is still the original.

NOTES (See Page 76.)

1. We started construction of our summer home at Camp Nelson in the summer of 1957. At that time money was scarce, and we did everything to economize.

That year demolition was started of the main building at Wasco Union High School which was constructed in 1915. The demolition company was salvaging most of the building materials and offered them for sale. learned about the materials and went to see if I could use some in building our summer home. I purchased

68 2" x 6" x 26' to be used as ceiling joists and rafters plus 3,000 board feet of 1" x 6" roof sheathing for $200. Today this lumber would run thousands of dollars.

At that time one of the clerks in the Pacific Gas & Electric Co. office where I was office supervisor had a father who was a retired carpenter. His name was Mr. Vernon Holland, and I hired him for two weeks to help me get started on our home. One day when looking at the 2" x 6" lumber I had purchased, Mr. Holland quipped, "Vernon, I will give you a dollar for every knot you can find in this lumber." Of course there weren't any. Then he also said, taking out his tape measure, "See, these are excellent. They measure a full 2" x 6" and not 1-1/2" x 5-1/2" like lumber today."

This wood must have been good because a few years later we had a snowstorm which dropped approximately 7' of snow on our roof without it sustaining any damage. Some of the other homes in the area were not so lucky; Their roofs collapsed and some had their homes completely destroyed.

ACKNOWLEDGMENTS

My heartfelt thanks to my younger daughter, Paula, who as a busy court reporter for Los Angeles County devoted weekend after weekend to help me complete this book. She, together with my wife, did most of the editing except where I purposefully left some of the slang and idioms intact, reserving all rights to veto their suggestions at my own discretion :)

NOTES

NOTES

NOTES

Printed in the United States
202270BV00002B/118-228/P